The Pig, or Václav Havel's Hunt for a Pig

and

Ela, Hela, and the Hitch

Book Design by Clinton Corbett

Also From Theater 61 Press:

Lysistrata
The Golem, Methuselah, Shylock: Plays
The Velvet Oratorio
Playing Dreidel With Judah Maccabee

THE HAVEL COLLECTION

The Memo
The Increased Difficulty of Concentration
The Vaněk Plays
Leaving
The Pig, or Václav Havel's Hunt for a Pig

To my collaborator, Henry Akona. As always, my work would not be the same without his input.

E. E.

The Pig, or Václav Havel's Hunt for a Pig

by

Václav Havel and
Vladimír Morávek

and

Ela, Hela, and the Hitch

by

Václav Havel

Translated by
Edward Einhorn
*From the literal translation
by Katerina Lu*

Theater 61 Press New York

Published by Theater 61 Press
A division of Untitled Theater Company #61
Manufactured in the United States of America
ISBN 0-9770197-9-9

TABLE OF CONTENTS

NOTE FROM DIVADLO HUSA NA PROVÁZKU

In the 2008-09 season, Divadlo Husa na Provázku Brno (Theatre Goose on a String, in Brno) produced the works of Václav Havel, an effort which culminated in the workshop production of CIRCUS Havel, or "We are all Lád'a," a four-hour–long montage incorporating Havel's complete works. The performance evoked a tremendous response both in the theater community and in the press, afterwards winning Divadelni Noviny's annual award.

While we were putting together this intense theatrical event, we discovered a rare text, which was not included in the final performance because of time restraints, but which we were overjoyed to find. It was a generally unknown piece call *The Pig*, which he based on apparently true events: an amusing story about how Havel, then a dissident, had tried to acquire a pig in a village far from Prague for a *zabíjačka*.* In this case, the *zabíjačka* is also an excuse for a gathering of friends and fellow dissidents.

The entire village is astir. Havel's involvement makes it both a political question, and, clearly, an opportunity to make a lot of money. And so an absurdist chain of events is unleashed. How can they deliver the pig (or not), whom to delegate for the delicate task of making the delivery, and most importantly how to make some profit.

All in all, the text is a combination of Hašek's comic grotesques and Kafka's senseless, aimless wandering through a world of the unutterable, the unnamable, and the ungraspable.

That this wonderful text is essentially unknown, only having been printed in the small periodical Nový Brak, Volume I, No. 10, makes its staging a remarkable event.

The sequence of cabarets in the production uses excerpts from the most famous of Czech operas, Smetana's *The Bartered Bride*. The main character of that opera, the Czech people, proclaim repeatedly in full choral voice: "Why not make a celebration/God has given us our health." This is the same mood one finds in Milos Forman's film, *The Firemen's Ball*; there, as well, the characters try clumsily to live in a state of bliss but instead ride off into the sunset feeling only awkwardness and embarrassment.

---

*The zabíjačka is a traditional Czech rural event, usually lasting a full day in late fall or early winter, in which a pig is slaughtered as part of a gathering of friends and family. The gathering centers around the preparation of the pig, accompanied by drinking, of course, and then the pig is eaten as part of a feast. Afterwards, the remainder is packaged and given to the celebrants as a present.

TRANSLATOR'S NOTE

This is not a play, exactly. Nor is it an operetta. It is a collage. An adaptation of an adaptation. A multimedia and multidisciplinary work culled from two different cultures and three centuries. Originally a short dialogue from 1987 and printed in a *samizdat*, or underground magazine (often photocopies of photocopies), the piece is a shaggy-dog tale at heart; a comic (and true) story of Havel's efforts to hold a pig roast for his friends. In 2010, Czech director Vladimír Morávek, of Theater Goose on the String, rediscovered the dialogue and decided to stage it. He began by giving lines to characters only mentioned in passing, but then made a more radical choice: he added sections from of one of the most beloved Czech works, *The Bartered Bride*.This new version was the centerpiece of a theater festival in Brno last June.

I was invited to attend the festival yet knew nothing about the piece before I arrived. Like many of Havel's plays, I see it as a veiled critique of the Communist system; however, *The Bartered Bride* adds another layer to the story. The operetta was written at a time (the 1860s) when the act of speaking Czech was, in itself, a nationalistic gesture. Spoken Czech had died out and Smetana, among others, wanted to restore it as a living language (and gain independence from the Austro-Hungarian Empire). In the context of *The Pig*, the celebratory music foreshadows the Velvet Revolution, the overthrow of Communism, and Havel's election to the presidency.

Indeed, near the end of the piece, Morávek slips the words "truth and love" into the lyrics; a reference to Havel's most famous quote, "Truth and love must prevail over lies and hatred." Upon seeing the production, I asked whether I could translate *The Pig* for a production here in New York. I cannot speak Czech. I have taken classes and done my best to learn it, but Czech, especially spoken Czech, eludes me. The sounds are very difficult for my ear, and I'm sure when I speak it, my accent is terrible. And so the title of translator seems a little suspicious to me.

But what I did was this: I worked with a native speaker, Katerina Lu, until I understood every nuance of the original. I took my notes and found ways to convey not only the meaning of the lines but also Havel's rhythms and wry humor.

I then started writing my own dialogue, particularly for the Journalist. The character's lines are in "English" in the original, but I altered the (technically correct) lines to sound natural to an American. And as I worked, I realized that common references for Czechs—the plot of *The Bartered Bride* or events of the Velvet Revolution—would be lost on most Americans.

I began adding lines to set up the play for a New York audience. Then, working with the director, Henry Akona, I added silent characters, partly to utilize 3LD Art + Technology's video capabilities and partly to echo the silent characters in many of Havel's other plays ... and then I played with the placement of choruses ... and added a few more lines, and...

In the end, this production takes the Brno script and augments it with our own creative imaginings, just as Havel's original was augmented by Morávek. To me, it has become something of a cross-cultural dialogue. What better way to work on a piece whose two main characters are an American and a Czech? But primarily, Havel himself is the main inspiration behind my efforts. *The Pig* is his only work in which he appears on stage as one of the characters. My challenge was to convey Havel's voice, which is witty, wise, sometimes a little testy, but always compassionate and humane.

Edward Einhorn

The Pig, or Václav Havel's Hunt for a Pig

by

Václav Havel and

Vladimír Morávek

The English-language premiere of *The Pig, or Václav Havel's Hunt for a Pig* was presented as part of the Ohio Theater's Ice Factory Festival. It played from June 29 – July 2, 2011, at the 3LD Art + Technology Center in New York City. It was produced by Untitled Theater Company #61.

PRODUCTION TEAM

DIRECTOR
Henry Akona

CHOREOGRAPHER
Patrice Miller

STAGE MANAGER
Elizabeth Irwin

ASSISTANT MUSICAL DIRECTOR
Melissa Elledge

ASSISTANT DIRECTOR
Joe Pilowski

DRAMATURG
Karen Lee Ott

SET DESIGNER
Jane Stein

LIGHTING DESIGNER
Jeff Nash

COSTUME DESIGNER
Carla Gant

PROJECTION DESIGNER
Kate Freer &
David Tennet

SOUND OPERATOR
Will Campbell

BAND COORDINATOR
Yvonne Roen

CAST/MUSICIANS

AMERICAN JOURNALIST......................Katherine Boynton
ACCORDION...Melissa Elledge
ENSEMBLE.........................Elizabeth Figols-Galagarza
KEŠOT/ENSEMBLE..................................John Gallop III
CAMERA OP.......................................Andrew Goldsmith
HAVEL..Robert Honeywell
FANDA/CHORAL
LEADER/TROMBONE...........................Michael Hopewell
VIOLIN...Amanda Lo
CELLO..Michael Midlarsky
TAP MASTER'S WIFE/
ENSEMBLE/CLARINET..........................Jenny Lee Mitchell
GRIP..Mateo Moreno

CAST/MUSICIANS (CONT'D.)

TOMAČKA/ENSEMBLE/VIOLIN....................Phoebe Silva

SOPRANO SOLOIST/ENSEMBLE....................Moira Stone

TENOR SOLOIST/ENSEMBLE......................Terrence Stone

TAP MASTER/ENSEMBLE........................Michael Whitney

OLGA/ENSEMBLE/FLUTE................................Sandy York

(L to R) Jenny Lee Mitchell, Michael Whitney, Robert Honeywell, Terrence Stone, Sandy York, Elizabeth Figols-Galagarza, Phoebe Silva, Moira Stone.

Katherine Boynton and cast. Photos by Edward Einhorn.

Act 1

(An AMERICAN JOURNALIST is
interviewing VÁCLAV HAVEL.
The CAMERMAN has her on camera
and will follow her throughout the show.
Also involved is a GRIP, a man in a cheap
suit who seems out of place. Occasionally
THE GRIP writes things in a small
notebook, in a vaguely ominous way.)

*In the New York production, a news crawl
occasionally appeared below the live feed
projections, as part of the live broadcast from the
fictional network, NNC. At this point, the crawl
included the following:*

HEADLINES:
*- Congressional committee prepares final report
on the Iran-Contra affair.*
*- Ronald Reagan nominates Douglas Ginsburg
to be the next Supreme Court Justice; Democrats
promise a battle.*
*- Gorbachev accused of fostering a cult of
personality at a party meeting to discuss
perestroika.*
*- Stock prices begin to recover after record
plunge.*
*- Soviets say antimissile system would give U. S.
a decisive military advantage.*

JOURNALIST

Good evening, ladies and gentleman. You are about to witness a strange and wonderful ritual of the Czech people, something that they call a zabishka.

(Listens at earpiece.)

Sorry, that is a…za-bee-yach-ka. A traditional Czech Pig Festival, in which a whole village comes together sometime in late autumn or early winter to celebrate the slaughter of a pig.

(Listens at earpiece.)

Sorry, I am told that it is a close group of friends and family who come together for a full day to celebrate the slaughter—

(Listens at earpiece.)

Yes, I see. It is not exactly the slaughter of the pig that is being celebrated. But a pig is involved. And it is slaughtered. And then prepared. And I'm pretty sure they eat it. There is a lot of beer drinking involved, that much I can say for sure. Listen now, as they sing a traditional zabíjačka song:

Chorus 1

CHOIR

WHY NOT MAKE A CELEBRATION?
WHY NOT MAKE A CELEBRATION?

GOD HAD GIVEN US OUR HEALTH, US OUR HEALTH.
GOD HAD GIVEN US OUR HEALTH, US OUR HEALTH.
GOD HAD GIVEN US OUR HEALTH, US OUR HEALTH.

THEY ARE HAPPY WHO KNOW HOW TO
    MAKE EACH SINGLE MINUTE COUNT,
    MINUTE COUNT.

(JOURNALIST listens at earpiece.)

JOURNALIST

I am being told that what we heard was actually
an excerpt from *The Bartered Bride*, a 19th century
Czech operetta. Still, it certainly is celebratory,
isn't it?

(Listens at earpiece.)

I am being told that I am not here to report on the
zabíjačka at all. I am here to interview Mr. Václav
Havel, a famous pig farmer.

(Listens at earpiece.)

I mean to say that Mr. Václav Havel is a famous
Czech playwright and one of the main figures
behind Charter 77, the human rights movement in
Czechoslovakia. Welcome, Mr. Havel.

HAVEL

Good afternoon.

JOURNALIST

Mr. Havel, I have heard that you were engaged in
trying to help a People's Self-Help Library known as
The Tomb.

(Listens at earpiece.)

For those watching, I want to mention that though the Self-Help Libraries are emblematic of the government's Communist ideals, this particular library has a reputation for being a harbor for dissidents. And you were organizing a zabíjačka for it, is this true?

HEADLINE:
- Self-Help Library a front for dissidents.

HAVEL

Yes, this is true. I was, for a certain period, involved in the effort to acquire a pig. I would like to emphasize that my participation was limited in time and limited to certain particular aspects of that effort.

Chorus 2

PIGS INSPIRE CELEBRATION, SOON WE'LL HAVE
    OUR ZABÍJAČKA.
PIGS INSPIRE CELEBRATION, SOON WE'LL HAVE
    OUR ZABÍJAČKA.
WIVES ARE IN THE KITCHENS COOKING,
HUSBANDS IN THE BACKROOMS DRINKING.

JOURNALIST

When exactly did this participation begin, Mr. Havel?

HAVEL

I started to involve myself at the point when I
realized that some pig farmers who had previously
pledged to donate a pig to the People's Self-
Help Library known as the Tomb had, at the last
moment, reneged on that promise in regard to the
aforementioned pig. They were probably afraid
that they might be linked to an event that might
in some way discredit them — in other words, a
zabíjačka at Havel's summer estate at Hrádeček.

Chorus 3

CHOIR

OH NO (OH NO) NO NO (NO NO) OH NO.
SOON OUR JOY WILL END, SOON OUR JOY
   WILL END.
WITH OUR CARES DESCENDING,
SOON OUR JOY WILL HAVE ITS ENDING.
IRATE, IRRITATED, IRATE, IRRITATED, IRATE,
   IRRITATED, IRRITATED.
OH NO...

JOURNALIST

What's this opera about?

HAVEL

It's about a Bartered Bride.

JOURNALIST

Oh...

CHOIR

THE NEXT PIG WILL COME, WHO KNOWS
   WHEN?
THE NEXT PIG WILL COME, WHO KNOWS
   WHEN?
SHALL WE BE SO HAPPY THEN, HAPPY THEN?
SHALL WE BE SO HAPPY THEN, HAPPY THEN?
SHALL WE BE SO HAPPY THEN, HAPPY THEN?

HAVEL

I felt like it would be a point of honor or personal prestige to demonstrate that I could find a way to overcome this very Czech tendency to shift ground whenever it seems expedient. But I did not then realize what was in store for me...

Chorus 4

IRATE, IRRITATED, IRATE, IRRITATED, IRATE,
   IRRITATED, IRRITATED.
OH NO...

JOURNALIST

But Mr. Havel, I am interested in knowing the exact moment when these incidents began.

HAVEL

Last Wednesday, when I visited the pub at Vlčice.

Chorus 5

JENÍK (TENOR)

WHY SO SAD AND FARAWAY, MY DARLING
   MAŘENKA?

MAŘENKA (SOPRANO)

I QUIVER WITH FEAR.
ALL NIGHT LONG I'VE HAD SUCH AWFUL
    DREAMS.
FOR WITHOUT A PIG OUR ZABÍJAČKA'S BOUND
    TO FAIL.

JOURNALIST

Here, the bride and her lover express their
deepest fears.

MAŘENKA (SOPRANO)

DEAR GOD, WHAT WILL HAPPEN?

JOURNALIST

Those fears are of course unfounded.

(JOURNALIST listens at earpiece.)

I'm sorry, I'm told everything goes terribly wrong.

JENÍK (TENOR)

COME NOW, THERE'S NO NEED TO FEAR,
    JUST REMEMBER I AM HERE.
YOU JUST NEED A WILL THAT'S FORGED FROM
    IRON, THEN WE WILL PREVAIL.
THEN WE WILL PREVAIL.

CHOIR

NO MORE TROUBLES, NO MORE SORROWS,
    NO MORE NEED FOR FEAR.
HOLD FAST ONTO YOUR CONVICTIONS,
    GIVEN TIME THEY'LL LEAD TO BLESSINGS.
IN TIME THEY WILL LEAD TO BLESSINGS.

WHY NOT MAKE A CELEBRATION?
WHY NOT MAKE A CELEBRATION?
GOD HAS GIVEN US OUR HEALTH,
    US OUR HEALTH.
GOD HAD GIVEN US OUR HEALTH,
    US OUR HEALTH.
GOD HAD GIVEN US OUR HEALTH,
    US OUR HEALTH.

THEY ARE HAPPY WHO KNOW HOW TO
MAKE EACH SINGLE MINUTE COUNT,
    MINUTE COUNT.
THEY ARE HAPPY WHO KNOW HOW TO
MAKE EACH SINGLE MINUTE COUNT,
    MINUTE COUNT;
MAKE EACH SINGLE MINUTE COUNT,
    MINUTE COUNT;
MAKE EACH SINGLE MINUTE COUNT.

HAVEL

Excuse me, tap master, sir, might you know, by any
chance, whether I could find any pigs in Vlčice?
The tap master replied:

TAP MASTER

Pigs? There are plenty of pigs, here. Someone or
other was trying sell his pig not long ago, but he

couldn't, not for 25 crowns a kilo. But here, a pig can always be acquired. I have a brother-in-law, for example, he would definitely sell you one. Named Lád'a. That's my brother-in-law's name, I mean.

HAVEL

That's when I made a fatal mistake. I said to the tap master: That's wonderful! We're definitely interested! 25 or 30 crowns per kilo, whatever the cost, that's fine with us, what's important is that we need to be sure about the pig.

Chorus 6

JENIK & MAŘENKA

IS IT POSSIBLE, CAN HE ACHIEVE THIS FEAT?

MAŘENKA

NEVER WOULD I HAVE BELIEVED IT TRUE,
   THAT A MAN COULD BE SO CLEVER.
YOU WILL BRING US BACK OUR PIG,
   SAVING OUR ENDEAVOR.

> (HAVEL attempts to leave, but the choir blocks him.)

CHOIR

Not quite yet sir, not quite yet sir, we are not quite finished yet, not yet.

JOURNALIST

Watch now, while this fateful document is signed,
the contact for the barter of the bride. I mean,
the pig.

TAP MASTER

IPSO FACTO, FOR THIS SMALL CONSIDERATION,
    FOR A BONA FIDE SUM IN COMPENSATION.
SUB NOMINE BOTH YOU AND ME
    AND THEN A PIG YOU WILL SEE.

HAVEL

And the price?

TAP MASTER

Thirty crowns.

HAVEL

(Spoken.)

Here is my signature, and today's date.

(ALL react with disappointment.
KEŠOT goes to get a script.)

What? What?

(KEŠOT shows him in the script.)

KEŠOT

You're supposed to sing it.

HAVEL

Sing it?

(KEŠOT nods.)

But I don't...I can't really —

KEŠOT

It's OK everyone, he's going to sing it.

(Everyone returns to stage. JOHN shows him
in the book and demonstrates.)

It's simple. Like this:

KEŠOT

(Sung.)

Here is my signature and today's date!

(HAVEL attempts to imitate.)

HAVEL

(Sung.)

Here is my signature, and today's date!

(HAVEL signs.)

Now I understand these men, and so I'm glad to
use my pen.

CHOIR

BOUGHT A PIG, BOUGHT A PIG, BOUGHT A PIG,
   BOUGHT A PIG
FOR THIRTY CROWNS.
AT LONG LAST WE HAVE OUR PIG.
IT SHALL NOT BE OVERPRICED.

BOUGHT A PIG, YES, BOUGHT A PIG, FOR JUST
   THIRTY CROWNS,
A PLUMP AND JUICY —
BOUGHT A PIG, YES WE BOUGHT A PIG,
   FOR JUST THIRTY CROWNS.
WE BOUGHT A BIG, FAT, HEALTHY PIG.

JOURNALIST

What happened next?

HEADLINES:
- *Miniskirts back in fashion.*
- Phantom of the Opera *prepares for Broadway run.*
- *Martina Navratilova edges out Chris Evert in finals.*
- *Fox Network premieres its first full season with* 21 Jump Street, Married With Children
- *Princess Diana rumored to being having an affair.*

(The actors enact the events as HAVEL
describes them.)

HAVEL

I came to an agreement with the tap master that a
friend of mine (by whom I mean Kešot) would visit
his fine establishment on Saturday and inquire as to
the progress of the pig situation. In the meanwhile,
I was obligated to go to Prague, where, as it
happens, I had duties both on the human rights
front and in my own apartment, where there were
contractors working.

JOURNALIST

What happened in the meantime? I mean, what happened in Vlčice while you were in Prague?

HAVEL

What happened was this: Kešot visited the tap master on Saturday, as arranged, and asked him how things were proceeding with the pig. The tap master told him that there were no problems vis a vis the pig, but the pig would be a bit smaller, and, naturally, more expensive, for it is not as economical to sell a small pig, making it necessary to price the pig at 40 crowns per kilo.

JOURNALIST

Any other developments?

HAVEL

On Sunday, things became complicated. A man arrived at Hrádeček who introduced himself as Fanda Vondráček. He appeared to be a tractor driver, and he had come to ask whether we were indeed looking for a pig, as he had heard. He knew further that we had received an offer of a pig, but it was an unworthy pig, and he said he could provide us with a pig that was really a pig. For a price, of course. He engaged in those negotiations with my friend Kešot and my wife, Olga.

Chorus 7

CHOIR

WHY NOT MAKE A CELEBRATION?
WHY NOT MAKE A CELEBRATION?
GOD HAS GIVEN US OUR HEALTH,
   US OUR HEALTH.
GOD HAD GIVEN US OUR HEALTH,
   US OUR HEALTH.
GOD HAD GIVEN US OUR HEALTH,
   US OUR HEALTH.
THEY ARE HAPPY WHO KNOW HOW TO
MAKE EACH SINGLE MINUTE COUNT,
   MINUTE COUNT.

JOURNALIST

How did the negotiations turn out?

HAVEL

In the end, we resolved to buy the bigger pig from him. Naturally, this was only on the condition that he was not trying to swindle the tap master who had originally promised us a pig, albeit a smaller pig than the one Fanda was offering. To which Fanda immediately replied:

FANDA

I will work it out with Láď'a and the tap master, don't worry, no problem.

Chorus 8

CHOIR

THEY ARE HAPPY WHO KNOW HOW TO
MAKE EACH SINGLE MINUTE COUNT,
  MINUTE COUNT;
MAKE EACH SINGLE MINUTE COUNT,
  MINUTE COUNT;
MAKE EACH SINGLE MINUTE COUNT.

JOURNALIST

Did anything else happen while you were
in Prague?

HAVEL

Later, Olga's grandniece Tomačka also came to
visit Hrádeček. Olga, in a sort of desperation
stemming from the politically driven rescindment
of our original pig agreement, had been making
efforts parallel to my own, and her grandniece
joyfully announced that she had a pig, as well. In
addition, this pig was the ideal weight, 150 kilos.
Naturally, this pig was located a distance away.
That was a definite disadvantage. It brought up
transportation issues. Moreover, we had already
received another guaranteed offer of a pig.
Therefore, Olga turned down her grandniece's pig,
deciding to depend instead on Fanda's pig, with
our backup pig being the one that the tap master's
brother-in-law Lád'a had guaranteed. Tomačka
was crestfallen, disappointed that she would have
to cancel her perfect pig deal. Before she left, we
checked in with the tap master, just to be sure.

To be honest, we weren't quite sure that Fanda's visit to Hrádeček and his activities in these pig matters weren't just some sort of side maneuver or scheme to undermine the tap master, and of course our first loyalty was to the tap master, not to Fanda, who was previously unknown to us. The tap master, on the other hand, was one of Vlčice's most important personalities, and we wanted remain on his good side. Finding the tap master was not so easy, of course. It was a Monday, so the pubs in Hrádeček were closed.

JOURNALIST

Why?

HAVEL

It's the day they close, since they're open weekends. There's not much you can do about that. But we finally found the tap master at his house in Vlčice.

Chorus 9

CHOIR

THEY ARE HAPPY WHO KNOW HOW TO
MAKE EACH SINGLE MINUTE COUNT,
    MINUTE COUNT;
MAKE EACH SINGLE MINUTE COUNT,
    MINUTE COUNT;
MAKE EACH SINGLE MINUTE COUNT.

HAVEL

He was lying underneath his car, and there was someone with him. This was his brother-in-law, Lád'a, there under the car as well.

JOURNALIST

Excuse me...is this the same Lád'a who owned the first pig?

HAVEL

Yes, that's exactly right, Lád'a, his brother-in-law, the owner of that self-same pig which we had come to reject because it was so small. We approached the car. We stood there for a moment. We said hello. From underneath the car came a voice:

TAP MASTER

Hold on.

HAVEL

A woman looked out from the house and asked:

WIFE

Milan! Who are these guys?

HAVEL

The tap master says:

TAP MASTER

Don't worry about it. Give me a minute, they'll be outta here.

HAVEL

After some time, the tap master crawled out from under the car, turned to us and said:

TAP MASTER

So, sorry to tell you, but as it turns out the pig's not for sale. It's a runt. Ain't worth nothing now, huh, Lád'a?

HAVEL

From underneath the car came:

LÁD'A

Yep, it's a runt, gotta grow.

Chorus 10

CHOIR

WHY NOT MAKE A CELEBRATION?

HAVEL

This was a completely unexpected turn of events. We had come to make excuses for rejecting the pig, and now it was apparent that we weren't going to get it, regardless.

CHOIR

WHY NOT MAKE A CELEBRATION?

So we assured the tap master that we had Fanda's
pig, which we could count on, and that we were
glad to hear that Fanda wasn't trying to swindle
Lád'a, whose pig was a runt and not yet full
grown, and —

CHOIR

THEY ARE HAPPY WHO KNOW HOW TO
MAKE EACH SINGLE MINUTE COUNT,
  MINUTE COUNT;
MAKE EACH SINGLE MINUTE COUNT,
  MINUTE COUNT;
MAKE EACH SINGLE MINUTE COUNT.

HAVEL

— and so, to put it simply, we left.

JOURNALIST

Well. That was on Monday, wasn't it? What
happened next?

HAVEL

Nothing on Tuesday.

JOURNALIST

Am I to understand that on Wednesday
something happened?

HAVEL

On Wednesday, there was a new, and
significant, setback.

Chorus 11

OH NO (OH NO) NO NO (NO NO) OH NO...
SOON OUR JOY WILL END, SOON OUR JOY
    WILL END.
WITH OUR CARES DESCENDING,
SOON OUR JOY WILL HAVE ITS ENDING.
IRATE, IRRITATED, IRATE, IRRITATED, IRATE,
    IRRITATED, IRRITATED.
OH NO...

HAVEL

We had planned to have an important discussion
with Fanda that day about the transportation and
delivery of Fanda's pig to our place in Hrádeček.

CHOIR

THE NEXT PIG WILL COME, WHO KNOWS
    WHEN?
THE NEXT PIG WILL COME, WHO KNOWS
    WHEN?
SHALL WE BE SO HAPPY THEN, HAPPY THEN?
SHALL WE BE SO HAPPY THEN, HAPPY THEN?
SHALL WE BE SO HAPPY THEN, HAPPY THEN?

HEADLINES:
- *Prague awaits the Glasnost Invasion.*
- *Judge Ginsburg admits to smoking marijuana
  in the '60s.*
- *Husak proposes broad changes for
  Czechoslovakia.*
- *Pork belly prices rise; oil down.*
- *Deficit inspires Thatcher pledge to trim the fat.*
- *Peasant dances become new craze!*

JOURNALIST

Now, if I understand you correctly, this is a very important moment in your story. Please be specific. We are very interested in this part of your story.

(The actors enact the story as HAVEL describes it.)

HAVEL

Yes, I will tell you precisely what happened. The first challenge in our venture was the finding of Fanda. First, he was supposedly in his workshop. Then, with the cows. Then, probably at home — though no one knew exactly where he lived, when we asked. Then, someone suggested that he might be out back. Then maybe out front with the pigs. Then with the Head of the Farming Collective. Finally, Fanda appeared, at our car.

Chorus 12

CHOIR

IRATE, IRRITATED, IRATE, IRRITATED, IRATE, IRRITATED, IRRITATED.
OH NO...

HAVEL

The second challenge was to agree upon a price. I asked: How much might it cost, per kilo?
And he said:

FANDA

If you ask me, I wouldn't sell it for less than 45.

HAVEL

Oh, I see, that's…that's a little…that's fine, I guess, sure. How much does it weigh, by the way?

FANDA

110.

HAVEL

And I exclaimed: Great, that's great. That's just what we need. I was delighted.

Chorus 13

CHOIR

PROČ BYCHOM SE NETĚŠILI, PROČ BYCHOM
　SE NETĚŠILI,
KDYŽ NÁM PÁNBŮH ZDRAVÍ DÁ, ZDRAVÍ DÁ,
KDYŽ NÁM PÁNBŮH ZDRAVÍ DÁ, ZDRAVÍ DÁ,
KDYŽ NÁM PÁNBŮH ZDRAVÍ DÁ!

JENOM TEN JE VPRAVDĚ ŠŤASTEN, KDO ŽIVOTA
　UŽÍVÁ, UŽÍVÁ.
JENOM TEN JE VPRAVDĚ ŠŤASTEN, KDO ŽIVOTA
　UŽÍVÁ, UŽÍVÁ,
　KDO ŽIVOTA UŽÍVÁ, UŽÍVÁ,
　KDO ŽIVOTA UŽÍVÁ.

HAVEL

So shall we give you a down payment, then?

FANDA

Nope.

Chorus 14

JENÍK (TENOR)

WHY SO SAD AND FARAWAY, MY DARLING
  MAŘENKA?

MAŘENKA (SOPRANO)

I QUIVER WITH FEAR.
ALL NIGHT LONG, I'VE HAD SUCH AWFUL
  DREAMS.
FOR WITHOUT A PIG, OUR ZABÍJAČKA'S BOUND
  TO FAIL.
DEAR GOD, WHAT WILL HAPPEN?

JOURNALIST

I remember this. This is where the lovers express
their deepest fears. Which all come true, right?

JENÍK (TENOR)

COME NOW, THERE'S NO NEED TO FEAR,
  JUST REMEMBER I AM HERE.
YOU JUST NEED A WILL THAT'S FORGED FROM
  IRON, THEN WE WILL PREVAIL.
THEN WE WILL PREVAIL.

CHOIR

NO MORE TROUBLES, NO MORE SORROWS,
  NO MORE NEED FOR FEAR.
HOLD FAST ONTO YOUR CONVICTIONS,
  GIVEN TIME THEY'LL LEAD TO BLESSINGS.
IN TIME, THEY WILL LEAD TO BLESSINGS.

HAVEL

So, shall we give you a down payment, then?

FANDA

Nope.

HAVEL

To tell you the truth, this filled me with total despair.

FANDA

That ain't the way it works, you give your money to Lád'a, not to me.

HAVEL

But Lád'a supposedly had nothing to do with this pig. Or so it had seemed to me, until that moment. Lád'a's pig was supposedly a runt, not yet full grown. So that's when Kešot and I decided to put our foot down. We said to Fanda:

KEŠOT

You said this pig was yours when you came to talk to us, didn't you?

HAVEL

That was a mistake, on our part. As soon as we said that, Fanda started to get very hazy and convoluted in his responses. He began telling us:

FANDA

I ain't got no pig. I got an 80 kilo one, but it's a runt. Still gotta grow.

Chorus 15

CHOIR

THE MUSIC STARTS TO GO ROUND AND
  ROUND, ROUND AND ROUND...

HAVEL

We understood, now, that there was some sort of game being played in Vlčice, and we were its victims.

JENÍK (TENOR)

WHY SO SAD AND FARAWAY, MY DARLING
  MAŘENKA?

MAŘENKA (SOPRANO)

I QUIVER WITH FEAR.
ALL NIGHT LONG, I'VE HAD SUCH AWFUL
  DREAMS.
FOR WITHOUT A PIG, OUR ZABÍJAČKA'S BOUND
  TO FAIL.
DEAR GOD, WHAT WILL HAPPEN?

JOURNALIST

Oh, I remember this —

HAVEL

Yes, I know.

JENÍK (TENOR)

COME NOW, THERE'S NO NEED TO FEAR, JUST
   REMEMBER I AM HERE.
YOU JUST NEED A WILL THAT'S FORGED FROM
   IRON, THEN WE WILL PREVAIL.
THEN WE WILL PREVAIL.

HAVEL

We needed to show some backbone. Stop messing
around with us, we said. Well, that's what we
would have said, but didn't because we were too
afraid. What we actually said was that we would
very much like to know who really owned the 110
kilo pig and whether we might, eventually, take
possession of it. Fanda, now totally pissed off,
said:

FANDA

Let me talk to the gypsy about it.

JOURNALIST

The gypsy? What gypsy is this?

(HAVEL shrugs.)

FANDA

I'll come round at five. What time is it?

HAVEL

Five minutes to five.

FANDA

So, then at six. Or seven, at the latest.

HAVEL

We were anxious. But we had no choice but to
wait. So we waited. Time crawled by —

Chorus 16

CHOIR

OH NO (OH NO) NO NO (NO NO) OH NO...
SOON OUR JOY WILL END, SOON OUR JOY
  WILL END.
WITH OUR CARES DESCENDING,
SOON OUR JOY WILL HAVE ITS ENDING.
IRATE, IRRITATED, IRATE, IRRITATED, IRATE,
  IRRITATED, IRRITATED.
OH NO...

OUVEJ OUVEJ OUVEJ,
KONEC RADOSTÍ, KONEC RADOSTÍ,
HRNOU SE STAROSTI, HRNOU SE STAROSTI,
ZLOSTI, MRZUTOSTI, ZLOSTI MRZUTOSTI,
  ZLOSTI MRZUTOSTI, MRZUTOSTI OUVEJ.

OH NO (OH NO) —

> (HAVEL cuts off singing, music becomes
> instrumental instead.)

HAVEL

We had to pee, we wanted to get inside where
it was warm, and we just wanted to give the
whole thing up, but we couldn't. First of all, in five
minutes, or more likely in an hour, or maybe two or
three at the most, there might, quite possibly,

though again possibly not, arrive Fanda and a gypsy, and they might be bringing us a pig, which could in all likelihood weigh 110 kilos—which is exactly the pig we needed, although in the worst-case scenario, they would explain to us that the gypsy's pig was a runt, but that...at 10 pm, it started to snow.

CHOIR

OH NO (OH NO) NO NO (NO NO) OH NO...
SOON OUR JOY WILL END, SOON OUR JOY
    WILL END.
WITH OUR CARES DESCENDING,
SOON OUR JOY WILL HAVE ITS ENDING.
IRATE, IRRITATED, IRATE, IRRITATED, IRATE,
    IRRITATED, IRRITATED.
OH NO...

HAVEL

And then it hailed. And then the tornado came...

HEADLINE:
- *Winter Storm Warning.*

JOURNALIST

Thank you, Mr. Havel, for your detailed account. That brings an end to our interview.

(JOURNALIST listens at earpiece.)

Sorry, just one final question: What do you think of Mr. Gorbachev?

(THE GRIP clears his throat, threateningly.
HAVEL catches his eye.)

HAVEL

No comment.

Act 2

HEADLINES:
- *American journalist loses her way in Czechoslovakia, found at pig farm.*
- *Obscure avant garde Czech playwright still basically unknown in United States.*
- *Crying woman found in woods babbling about pigs.*
- *10 new ways to prepare ham!*
- *Inexplicable singing continues at country estate.*

JOURNALIST

We visited a close collaborator of Mr. Havel's, Mr. Kešot, and we asked him one question: Mr. Kešot, what do you think of this whole story?

KEŠOT

You were asking about Mr. Gorbachev.
If, regarding this, I could possibly comment...

> (THE GRIP steps towards KEŠOT. KEŠOT breaks off.)

JOURNALIST

Thanks anyway, Mr. Kešot! Now, we'd like to have a word with Mrs. Olga Havel. Mrs. Havel! Mrs. Havel! Mrs. Havlova!!! Where are you? Something must have happened! I heard someone crying...

> (JOURNALIST discovers HAVEL, with relief.)

Oh! Here's Mr. Havel! Good afternoon,
Mr. Havel. We wanted to speak with your wife...
What happened? Where is she?

HAVEL

I had a dream in which she ran into the woods.
Um...

JOURNALIST

I heard someone crying. Was it her?

HAVEL

Yes, she was crying, weeping inconsolably.
And what is this? Look, here's a note, with her
handwriting. Her writing looks shaky.

OLGA

I am distraught, disappointed, disillusioned,
disgruntled, dissatisfied, discombobulated,
disturbed, and disgusted...I simply have no words.

JOURNALIST

That's all?

HAVEL

It seems like that's everything.

Chorus 17

JENÍK (TENOR)

WHY SO SAD AND FARAWAY, MY DARLING
MAŘENKA?

MAŘENKA (SOPRANO)

I QUIVER WITH FEAR.
ALL NIGHT LONG I'VE HAD SUCH AWFUL
    DREAMS
FOR WITHOUT A PIG, OUR ZABÍJAČKA'S
    BOUND TO FAIL.
DEAR GOD, WHAT WILL HAPPEN?

HAVEL

Wait, I've found another three sentences.

OLGA

You pork rind! Ham hock! Bacon bit!

(MAŘENKA flees. JENÍK turns to comfort
HAVEL instead.)

HEADLINES:
- Bartered bride breakup?
- Mařenka deepest secrets revealed.
- Jeník declare prague's most eligible batchelor.
- Smetana operetta a smash hit!

JENÍK (TENOR)

COME NOW, THERE'S NO NEED TO FEAR,
    JUST REMEMBER I AM HERE.
YOU JUST NEED A WILL THAT'S FORGED FROM
    IRON, THEN WE WILL PREVAIL.
THEN WE WILL PREVAIL.

CHOIR

NO MORE TROUBLES, NO MORE SORROWS,
 NO MORE NEED FOR FEAR.
HOLD FAST ONTO YOUR CONVICTIONS,
 GIVEN TIME THEY'LL LEAD TO BLESSINGS.
IN TIME THEY WILL LEAD TO BLESSINGS.

HAVEL

Fuck off, all of you!

JOURNALIST

Thank you, Mr. Havel! Since we have this splendid
opportunity to speak with you some more, could
you tell us what finally happened yesterday
evening? For our viewers: we are talking to Mr.
Václav Havel, a very important Czechoslovak
dissident playwright. Please, continue with what
happened, Mr. Havel.

HAVEL

My apologies. Let me do my best to explain exactly
what happened. Nothing. Nothing happened.
Fanda and the gypsy did not come, not at five,
nor at six, nor seven, nor eight, nor nine, nor even
at ten. And so we headed to bed, disappointed
and feeling like incompetents. Easy marks.
Complete failures.

> (Chaos ensues during Chorus 18. We are
> in a mishmash of moments within the play,
> which can either be interpreted as Havel's
> nightmare or a Havellian "hubbub.")

HEADLINES:
- *Pig admits to smoking marijuana.*
- *Martina Navrotilova defeats Ronald Reagan in Wimbledon finals.*
- *Princess Diana having an affair with bartered bride!*
- *Phantom of the Opera a front for dissidents.*
- *Thatcher wears miniskirt.*
- *Gorbachev guest stars on 21 Jump Street.*
- *Winter Opera Warning!*

Chorus 18

CHOIR

PROČ BYCHOM SE NETĚŠILI, PROČ BYCHOM SE
NETĚŠILI.
KDYŽ NÁM PÁNBŮH ZDRAVÍ DÁ, ZDRAVÍ DÁ,
KDYŽ NÁM PÁNBŮH ZDRAVÍ DÁ, ZDRAVÍ DÁ,
KDYŽ NÁM PÁNBŮH ZDRAVÍ DÁ, ZDRAVÍ DÁ.

JENOM TEN JE VPRAVDĚ ŠŤASTEN,
KDO ŽIVOTA UŽÍVÁ, UŽÍVÁ.

JOURNALIST

And what happened today? This morning?

HAVEL

This morning we got up, bleary eyed and at a
complete loss. We were expecting a number of
guests, and we did not have a pig.

Chorus 19

CHOIR

OH NO (OH NO) NO NO (NO NO) OH NO...

HAVEL

We had no idea what to do. So we just hid
ourselves away, each in our own room, staring into
the emptiness. This, quite suddenly, was the end
of our being able to believe in anything. So noted
in Czechoslovakia, in the Year of our Lord, one
thousand nine hundred and eighty seven.

JOURNALIST

And now it's 4:25 in the afternoon.
What's happened between then and now?

HAVEL

At five minutes after twelve, guess who appears
behind our garden gate, smiling a brilliant smile?
Fanda!

Chorus 20

CHOIR

WHY NOT MAKE A CELEBRATION!

HAVEL

He comes with joyful news.

FANDA

Mám Prase!

HAVEL

Do you understand?

JOURNALIST

(Not understanding.)

I do.

FANDA

I've got a pig!

JOURNALIST

Oh, yes!

HAVEL

This time, Fanda had truly found us a pig, although it was for an astronomical price.

Chorus 21

CHOIR

TELL US, OH VILLAGERS, WHAT DID YOU DO?
TELL, TELL.WHAT DID YOU DO?
TELL, TELL. WHAT DID YOU DO?
SO THAT THIS STORY ENDS CHEERFULLY,
    ENDS CHEERFULLY.
SO THAT THIS STORY ENDS CHEERFULLY.
TELL US, OH VILLAGERS, WHAT DID YOU DO?
    TELL, TELL.
TELL US JUST WHAT DID YOU DO?
TELL US JUST WHAT DID YOU DO?
    OH PLEASE DO TELL.

OLGA

One hundred crowns per kilo?

HAVEL

It was a price beyond all expectation.

OLGA

One ten?

HAVEL

A price I can't even utter.

OLGA

One fifty?

HAVEL

A price that far exceeded even the wildest imaginings of the participants in the feast.

OLGA

Two hundred per kilo?

Chorus 22

CHOIR

TELL US, OH VILLAGERS, WHAT DID YOU DO?
  TELL, TELL.
TELL US JUST WHAT DID YOU DO?

HAVEL

It was a price, which, of course, we had to agree to, if we wanted to have any pig at all.

CHOIR

TELL US JUST WHAT DID YOU DO?
OH PLEASE DO TELL.

(Whispers something to OLGA.)

OLGA

But that's unheard of!

HAVEL

Naturally, we agreed to it.

OLGA

I don't think one should agree to a price like that.

HAVEL

Thank you, thank you, a thousand times thank you.

(Mumbles.)

I'll take it.

OLGA

Václav, please, no!

HAVEL

Yes! The villagers of Vlčice had succeeded in
their game!

Chorus 23

FANDA

PUNCTUM SATIS, SOTTO VOCE, SINE DIE, NOW
THE DEAL IS DONE.

HAVEL

Let's sign on this awful business Three hundred
crowns it is. Here is my signature...and today's
date!

(HAVEL signs.)

CHOIR

BOUGHT A PIG, BOUGHT A PIG, BOUGHT A PIG,
  BOUGHT A PIG.
FOR THREE HUNDRED.
AT LONG LAST WE HAVE OUR PIG.
IT SHALL NOT BE OVERPRICED.
BOUGHT A PIG, BOUGHT A PIG,
  FOR THREE HUNDRED CROWNS.
A TINY, LITTLE RUNT.
BOUGHT A PIG, YES WE BOUGHT A PIG,
  THREE HUNDRED CROWNS.
WE BOUGHT A TINY, LITTLE RUNT.
OH GLORY, GLORY, GLORY, GLORY, GLORY,
  GLORY, GLORY, OH SHAME!

(HAVEL takes the contract shows it to the
camera. He clearly has written "Protest" on
the cover.)

HAVEL

Now I understand these men, and so I'm glad
to use my pen.

(He hands the signed document to THE
GRIP, who realizes with horror what the
document is.)

HEADLINE:
- *Václav Havel and fellow dissidents present
formal protest on human rights to Czechoslovak
government officials.*

JOURNALIST

Thank you very much, Mr. Havel, for your account.

(Listens to earpiece.)

I'm sorry, if you don't mind, we have one last
question. It really is the final question. What do
you think about perestroika and the possibility
of reform in Czechoslovakia? What do you think
Husák will do?

HAVEL

~~Censored.~~

(HAVEL begins to respond, but THE GRIP
angrily pulls the cord, disconnecting the
camera signal.)

Chorus 24

CHOIR

WHAT A GOOD THING WE SUCCEEDED.
WHAT A GOOD THING WE SUCCEEDED.
TRUTH AND LOVE ARE UNIMPEDED.
TRUTH AND LOVE ARE UNIMPEDED.
HAPPINESS AND VICTORY!
HAPPINESS AND VICTORY!
HOW MERRY THIS FEAST WILL BE!
—THIS FEAST WILL BE...

> (ALL turn towards JOURNALIST. She realizes
> she's expected to sing.)

Chorus 25

JOURNALIST

NEVER WOULD I HAVE BELIEVED IT TRUE,
THAT A MAN COULD BE SO CLEVER.
YOU HAVE BROUGHT THEM BACK THEIR PIG,
SAVING THEIR ENDEAVOR.

> (JOURNALIST listens at earpiece.)

JOURNALIST

Wait, Mr. Havel? I am being told I wasn't supposed
to ask you about the zabíjačka at all,
I was supposed to be asking you about the
political situation here in Czechoslovakia.
What do you think is going to happen
to you and your dissident friends?

> (JOURNALIST listens at earpiece again.)

What was that document you were signing?
What is a dissident? Was this story a commentary
on Communism?

> (JOURNALIST listens at earpiece again.)

Could there be a revolution here? Who would lead
it? What would happen afterwards? What will
happen to you? What will happen to your country?

> (THE JOURNALIST and CAMERAMAN get
> swept up into the dance.)

Chorus 26

CHOIR

WHY NOT MAKE A CELEBRATION?
WHY NOT MAKE A CELEBRATION?
GOD HAS GIVEN US OUR HEALTH, US OUR HEALTH.
GOD HAD GIVEN US OUR HEALTH, US OUR HEALTH.
GOD HAD GIVEN US OUR HEALTH, US OUR HEALTH.

PIGS INSPIRE CELEBRATION, SOON WE'LL HAVE
    OUR ZABÍJAČKA.
PIGS INSPIRE CELEBRATION, SOON WE'LL HAVE
    OUR ZABÍJAČKA.
WIVES ARE IN THE KITCHENS COOKING,
    HUSBANDS IN THE BACKROOMS DRINKING.

OH NO (OH NO) NO NO (NO NO) OH NO...
SOON OUR JOY WILL END, SOON OUR JOY
    WILL END.
WITH OUR CARES DESCENDING,

SOON OUR JOY WILL HAVE ITS ENDING.
IRATE, IRRITATED, IRATE, IRRITATED,
    IRATE, IRRITATED, IRRITATED.
OH NO...

WHY NOT MAKE A CELEBRATION?
WHY NOT MAKE A CELEBRATION?
GOD HAS GIVEN US OUR HEALTH, US OUR HEALTH.
GOD HAD GIVEN US OUR HEALTH, US OUR HEALTH.
GOD HAD GIVEN US OUR HEALTH.

THEY ARE HAPPY WHO KNOW HOW TO
MAKE EACH SINGLE MINUTE COUNT,
    MINUTE COUNT.
THEY ARE HAPPY WHO KNOW HOW TO
MAKE EACH SINGLE MINUTE COUNT,
    MINUTE COUNT;
MAKE EACH SINGLE MINUTE COUNT,
    MINUTE COUNT;
MAKE EACH SINGLE MINUTE COUNT!

Chorus 27 [Curtain Call]

CHOIR
WHAT A GOOD THING WE SUCCEEDED.
WHAT A GOOD THING WE SUCCEEDED.
TRUTH AND LOVE ARE UNIMPEDED.
TRUTH AND LOVE ARE UNIMPEDED.
TRUTH AND LOVE...

(In the New York production, director
Henry Akona ended the show with
a graphic of Havel's signature, over
the bows.)

Ela, Hela, and the Hitch

by

Václav Havel

TRANSLATOR'S NOTE

Ela, Hela, and the Hitch was, in a way, Havel's first play. It was written for the Artistic Director of the Theatre on the Balustrade, Ivan Vyskočil, as part of a longer evening, entitled *Hitchhiking*. Prior to this play, Havel had worked mostly as a stagehand, and this was his first opportunity at any theater as a writer. Along with *Ela, Hela, and the Hitch*, he also wrote a sketch called *Motormorphosis*. Reportedly, Vyskočil altered Havel's sketches for the performance, though this text is Havel's original.

After Havel's success with his first full length, *The Garden Party*, these earlier efforts were quickly forgotten. They were relatively recently rediscovered, through the detective work of a Czech theater scholar, Lenka Jungmannová. *Motormorphosis* was performed at the Havel Festival in 2006, a world premiere of the text as written. *Ela, Hela, and the Hitch* premiered in English translation following a revival of *Motormorphosis* at New York's Bohemian National Hall in 2011.

What is particularly interesting about *Ela, Hela, and the Hitch* is the way it lays bare Ionesco's influence on Havel. The rhythms of the play echo everything from *The Bald Soprano* to *Salutations*. Like Ionesco, Havel uses comic repetition that culminates in an explosion of language, during which words become meaningless, replaced only by the more visceral meaning one can attach to pure sound.

Another interesting side note is the societal conflict reflected in the main dilemma. Like many older members of the Czechoslovak upper middle class in 1961 (the year the play was written), Ela and Hela spoke German at school, and their behavior is definitely reflective of the German influence on their upbringing. They are separated from society not only because of their age, but because the younger generation had cut its ties with Germany.

So what Havel is doing is using Ionesco's formal techniques, which Ionesco used primarily to critique humanity's doomed attempts at communication, and applying those techniques to a societal critique. Which is, in fact, a prelude to what Havel would do throughout the rest of his playwriting career.

Edward Einhorn

The English-language premiere of *Ela, Hela, and the Hitch* was presented as a staged reading at The Bohemian National Hall in New York City on June 15, 2011. It was produced by the Untitled Theater Company #61 and the Czech Center New York.

PRODUCTION TEAM

DIRECTOR	LIGHTING DESIGNER	STAGE MANAGER
Tom Berger	Jeff Nash	Berit Johnson

CAST

HELA...Uma Incrocci

ELA..Yvonne Roen

DRIVER....................................Andrew Schecheter

Act 1

(ELA and HELA, two elderly ladies, are
strolling on a road.)

ELA

Listen, Hela.

HELA

What is it, Ela?

ELA

That Lída of ours, right?

HELA

Yes...

ELA

Well, anyway, it's a wonderful thing, the way
we are able to sacrifice ourselves for our loved
ones, right?

HELA

Yes...

ELA

The way we are able to swallow our pride for the
sake of someone else.

HELA

Yes...

ELA

And do you know how we can do that?

HELA

Yes?

ELA

It is because of our ethical principles.

HELA

Mmm hmm.

ELA

Our human dignity.

HELA

Mmm hmm.

ELA

Our good upbringing.

HELA

Mmm hmm.

ELA

Our position in society.

HELA

Mmm hmm, Ela. Not just anyone could manage
that, the things we manage.

ELA

Not Karel, right?

HELA

Never Karel.

ELA

Not Jiřina either, right?

HELA

Never Jiřina.

ELA

And definitely not Osvald, right?

HELA

Never Osvald!

ELA

Never, none of them would be able to manage it.
And you know why that is?

HELA

Yes?

ELA

It is because they don't have their ethical
principles...

HELA

Right?

ELA

Their human dignity...

HELA

Right?

ELA

Their good upbringing...

HELA

Right?

ELA

Their position in society.

HELA

Mmm hmm. You see, it is we, with our position...

ELA

Upbringing...

HELA

Mmm hmm. With our dignity...

ELA

And principles...

HELA

Mmm hmm —with all that, we can manage to swallow our pride, take to the road, and hitchhike.

ELA

And sacrifice ourselves like that for our loved ones.

HELA

That Lída of ours...

ELA

Wait and see, after today, everything will be different...once we've experienced hitchhiking for ourselves.

HELA

Wait and see, we'll find out what sort of people take strange girls into their cars...

ELA

Wait and see, we'll know how to deal with that niece, that Lída of ours.

HELA

Mmm hmm.

ELA

What do you think, do these people have any ethical principles at all?

HELA

Certainly not.

ELA

Or any human dignity?

                    HELA

Never that.

                    ELA

Or any upbringing?

                    HELA

Never that, not ever.

                    ELA

Or any position in society?

                    HELA

Position? My girl, God knows what sort of people
they are.

                    ELA

And God knows what they're after.

                    HELA

God knows, my girl, God knows.

                    ELA

God knows...but, we are fearless, right?

                    HELA

Right?

                    ELA

Listen, there's something strange about this whole
hitchhiking thing, isn't there?

HELA

They're common riffraff.

ELA

Definitely!

HELA

Definitely!

ELA

We'll see it ourselves, now, with our own eyes.

HELA

Definitely...

ELA

Definitely...Listen, Hela

HELA

Definitely...What it it, Ela?

ELA

How is it that nobody has stopped for us yet,
considering that we've been hitchhiking for a few
hours now?

HELA

That's clear, after all! As soon as you look at us,
you can see that we have our ethical principles.

ELA

Our ethical principles, right?

HELA

And our human dignity.

ELA

Our human dignity, right?

HELA

And our good upbringing.

ELA

Our good upbringing, right?

HELA

And our position in society.

ELA

Our position in society, right?

HELA

Mmm hmm ....oh, that Lída of ours.

ELA

Listen, Hela.

HELA

What is it, Ela?

ELA

If nobody stops for us, then we will never actually experience hitchhiking.

HELA

What's that? You wouldn't actually want to go driving with them, in the end?

ELA

God forbid! I have my ethical principles, after all...and my human dignity...and my good upbringing...and my position in society...I only thought that if somebody should stop for us, we could see him from up close.

HELA

And perhaps we could spit in his face...

ELA

Yes, we could do that at some point...

HELA

But how we can get somebody to stop for us?

ELA

We have to look a little less serious, a little more like those modern floozies.

                    HELA

Perhaps we could sing, what do you think?

>   (They sing "Pisne, dcery ducha mehoof"
>   or "Songs, Daughters of my Soul", an old
>   traditional religious and patriotic song.)

                    ELA

Nothing, right?

                    HELA

Nothing.

                    ELA

Hmmm.

                    HELA

Hmmm.

                    ELA

Let's try to hop around as well...

                    HELA

Ela!

                    ELA

Just a little bit...a little tiny bit...

>   (They hop.)

                    HELA

Again, nothing, right? So, I don't know anymore.

ELA

Probably there's a special trick to it.

HELA

Probably.

ELA

Probably, I'm sure that there's a special trick to it.

HELA

Probably, there must exist a special trick to it.

ELA

Right? Probably there is. Some special trick.

HELA AND ELA

Trick, right? Trick, right?

> (ELA tries some different "tricks" while HELA
> watches closely.)

HELA

Listen, Ela

ELA

What is it, Hela?

HELA

Admit it, this whole thing excites you a little.

ELA

What's that, Hela?!

HELA

Admit it, this is just the type of adventure that you
are drawn to.

ELA

Excuse me, Hela?!

HELA

Admit it, this is the self-same false romanticism that
I used to always help you to overcome, when were
young.

ELA

You know very well it repulses me and that I am
only doing this as a sacrifice for the people I love.
Oh, that Lída of ours...but after all, we have our
ethical principles, our human dignity, our good
upbringing, and our position in society!

HELA

You're a lifelong romantic.

ELA

You say this, you! Like I don't know you! Or do
you think that I've forgotten, for example, the
Spring of 1910, in Brno, when the whole Vesna
Academy for Young Ladies was whispering about
your relationship to Professor Přibský? And do
you think that I don't remember how, to avoid
a scandal, Přibský was transferred to Vienna,
to the Allgemeine Bürgerliche Mädchenschule,
Hasenstraße Sechzehn.

HELA

Dreizehn... Ela! After all, you promised me that
you would never say that name in front of me, ever
again! And now this! Very well, then!

ELA

Sechzehn... So you see! That was not romantic,
right? A sixteen-year-old tadpole of a girl and Mr.
Professor! Yes?

HELA

Dreizehn! My feelings for Roman were clearly
a girlish infatuation for which I have never been
ashamed, though I don't know if you could say the
same about, for example, your relationship with
Professor Žahour! It's enough after all to remember
Profeesor Žahour's poem, printed by the Modern
Revue: "I am dipping my piccolo of passion/into
your corporeal creek."

ELA

Sechzehn! Hela, you are very cruel and cynical.
You should be ashamed of yourself. Didn't you
promise me that you world never remind me of
Otakar's name?

HELA

Dreizehn! You did it to me, so now you get you
just desserts. And I say again: Žahour.

ELA

So that's the way you want to be? Very well, then:
Přibský!

HELA

Ha! Žahour! Žahour!

ELA

Ha! Přibský! Přibský! Přibský!

HELA

Ha! Žahour! Žahour! Žahour! Žahour!

ELA

Ha! Přibský! Přibský! Přibský! Přibský! Přibský!

HELA

Žahour!

ELA

Přibský!

HELA

And I'm not even going into your afternoons at the ice rink with that student, Balda.

ELA

Better to spend afternoons at the ice rink with that student Balda then to spend evenings out of town with that reporter, Kopřiva.

HELA

Balda was a drop out.

ELA

Kopřiva was a paper pusher.

HELA

Anyway, I know who gave you that book of
Heyduk's poems.

ELA

And do you think that I don't know who gave you
that book of Joža Úprka's paintings?

HELA

Anyway, I know why you always make donuts on
the 20th of June!

ELA

And do you think I don't know why you have that
porcelain statue of a deer on your piano?

HELA

And what about Čipera?

ELA

And what about Machoň?

HELA

And what about Veverka?

ELA

And what about Pokorný?

HELA

Don't talk about Pokorný!

ELA

Pokorný! Pokorný!

HELA

Veverka! Veverka!

ELA

Machoň! Machoň!

HELA

Čipera! Čipera!

ELA

Kopřiva! Kopřiva!

HELA

Balda! Balda!

ELA

Přibský! Přibský!

HELA

Žahour! Žahour!

ELA

Přibský! Kopřiva! Machoň! Pokorný!

HELA

Žahour! Balda! Čipera! Veverka!

ELA

Přibský! Pokorný! Sechzehn!

HELA

Žahour! Veverka! Dreizehn!

ELA

Hela, we shouldn't tease each other like this!
We have our ethical principles!

HELA

You're right! And our human dignity!

ELA

Mmm hmm. And our good upbringing!

HELA

Mmm hmm. And our position in society!

ELA

Besides, our life, dear Hela, was never easy.

HELA

It was no bed of roses.

ELA

Life was never kind to us.

ELA

And you see, despite all that, we managed to keep
our ethical principles.

ELA

And our human dignity!

HELA

And our good upbringing!

ELA

And our position in society!

HELA

And we always sacrificed ourselves for our
loved ones.

ELA

Even though life was never kind to us.

HELA

Even though life was never a bed of roses,
not for us.

ELA

Even though our life was, quite simply, never easy.

HELA

If only everybody could be like us, my girl.

ELA

Then the world would never be at war, right?

HELA

Never, certainly. What if we try just one more trick: singing and hopping simultaneously...

ELA

Hela!

HELA

I know...just a little...

(They sing and hop.)

HELA

Nothing, right?

ELA

Nothing?

HELA

Those people have no ethical principles.

ELA

Nor any human dignity!

HELA

Nor any good upbringing!

ELA

Nor any position in society!

HELA

They let us stand here by the ditch like a couple
of wet hens.

ELA

And we sacrificed ourselves so much for our
loved ones.

HELA

And nobody cares for us!

ELA

Only Žahour cared for us…and who knows if…

HELA

Only Přibský…and who knows if…

ELA

Only Balda…and who knows if…

HELA

Only Kopřiva…and who knows if…

ELA

Only Čipera…and who knows if…

HELA

Only Machoň…and who knows if…

ELA

Only Veverka…and who knows if…

HELA

Only Pokorný...and who knows if...

ELA

They would have certainly stopped for us!

HELA

Přibský, Kopřiva, Machoň, and Pokorný, for sure...

ELA

Žahour, Balda, Čipera, and Veverka wouldn't even think twice about it

HELA

Oh dear God, Jóža Úprka!

ELA

Oh dear God, Adolf Heyduk!

HELA

Oh dearie goodness, donuts on the 20th of June.

ELA

Oh dearie dear, the porcelain deer!

HELA

And the porcelain Sechzehn!

ELA

And the porcelain Dreizehn!

                    HELA

And after all that, we didn't die.

                     ELA

We didn't, did we?

                    HELA

Ela...look...a car stopped!

          (They look backstage.)

                     ELA

Go to him!

                    HELA

What me? You go!

                     ELA

Should I spit in his face?

                    HELA

Hold off on that for now...until we see how
he looks.

          (DRIVER enters.)

                     ELA

What do you think, how does he look?

                    HELA

Hard to say...say something to him!

ELA

You fellow there, mind your manners!

(Whispers to HELA.)

Well?

HELA

Mmmm hmmm.

ELA

What do you actually think about us? Well?

HELA

Good, good...just continue!

ELA

What do you think we are, floozies?

HELA

Some kind of common riffraff?

ELA

You can't just come on to us, you should be ashamed!

HELA

Oh, that Lída of ours...

DRIVER

Good day, ladies! I'm afraid there's been a
bit of a misunderstanding. I did not actually
stop for you, but just sort of...I would say...by
accident...you see, to be exact, out of necessity...
you know how it suddenly comes on...

ELA

So you didn't stop for us? You see what you are
like! Oh, Hela dear, we are alone in the world!

HELA

And we have made so many sacrifices in our life!

DRIVER

If you allow me, ladies, I would like to mention, if
I might, that I couldn't very well stop for you, since
you didn't put out your thumb, after all...

HELA

What?

DRIVER

Since you didn't put out your thumb...

ELA

What?

DRIVER

I only wanted to let you know that you didn't put
out your thumb...

HELA

Excuse me, how dare you?

ELA

Us, put out our thumbs! That's the limit!

HELA

Put out our thumbs! Us! A trick like that!

ELA

Are we some kind of floozies?

HELA

Some kind of common riffraff?

ELA

And if you want to know something, we never in our life have put out our thumbs to anybody! Never in our life, sir! Never!

HELA

And we also will not put out our thumbs, sir, never in our life, never!

DRIVER

Well then, it might also be expected that, in all likelihood, never in your life will anybody stop.

HELA

Sir! We have our ethical principles!

                    ELA

Our human dignity!

                    HELA

Our good upbringing!

                    ELA

Our position in society!

                    HELA

Our good habits and practices!

                    ELA

Our family traditions!

                    HELA

Our heirlooms, memories, and idealism!

                    ELA

Our honor, name, and spotless reputation!

                    HELA

Our nieces, ancestors, and relatives!

                    ELA

Our loved ones and all those we hold dear!

                    HELA

Our Žahours and our Přibskýs

ELA

Our Kopřivas and Baldas!

HELA

Our Čiperas and Machoňs!

ELA

Our Veverkas and Pokornýs!

HELA

Our Heyduks and Úprkas!

ELA

Our donuts on the 20th of June!

HELA

Our porcelain deers!

ELA

Our coziness and cleanliness!

(Their speed and volume increase.)

HELA

Our laces, flags, and maladies!

ELA

Our ponderings, quills, and almanacs!

HELA

Our canaries, uncles, and dream books!

ELA

Our dressers and headboards!

HELA

Our bedspreads and breviaries!

ELA

Our softcover stories!

HELA

Our slippers!

ELA

Our sagas!

HELA

Our caddies and our granddaddies!

ELA

Our diaries, dusters, and dumplings!

HELA

Our smocks, our ills, our boxes of pills!

ELA

Our hats with veils, apron string tails, and all our travails.

HELA

Our potted plants, cabbage cooked, and fish filleted.

ELA

Our miniatures, models, and magpies.

HELA

Our perseverance, purses, and purchases!

(At maximum speed and volume.)

ELA

Our shangarisms, shantisms, and sharpisms

HELA

Our flamology, kastology, and zootopimology!

ELA

Our bladdence, kandary, and mardom.

HELA

Our sarbity, gyrodence, and mortness.

ELA

Our canapacy, candamence, and combring.

HELA

Look, Ela, he left...

ELA

You see...he certainly would not have left Lída!

HELA

Certainly not!

ELA

Oh, that Lída of ours!

HELA

What do we have in this life?

ELA

Only our ethical principles...

HELA

Only our human dignity...

ELA

Only our good upbringing...

HELA

Only our position in society...

ELA

Only our good upbringing...

HELA

Only our position in society...

ELA

Only our ethical principles...

HELA

Only our good upbringing...

ELA

Only our ethical principles...

HELA

Only our ethical principles...

ELA

Only our ethical principals...

> (The dialogue gets very quiet and the
> speed slows down.)

HELA

Only our human dignity...

ELA

Only our ethical principles...

HELA

Only our good upbringing...

ELA

Only our human dignity...

HELA

Only our position in society...

ELA

Only our ethical principles...

HELA

Only our position in society...

ELA

Only our good upbringing...

> (etc...The dialogue slowly changes into
> a whisper, becoming increasingly quiet
> until it is reduced to just movements
> and gestures, finally becoming
> complete calmness and silence.)

EDWARD EINHORN BIOGRAPHY

Edward Einhorn is the Artistic Director of Untitled Theater Company #61. With the company, he curated the Václav Havel Festival, the Ionesco Festival, the NEUROfest, and the Festival of Jewish Theater and Ideas, among other events. Other projects include: *The Velvet Oratorio*, an oratorio commemorating the 20th anniversary of the Velvet Revolution, produced at Lincoln Center and The Bohemian National Hall (librettist); *Rudolf II*, a play about the 16th-century Emperor in Prague produced at the Bohemian National Hall (playwright); the Off-Broadway production of *Fairy Tales of the Absurd* (writer and director); stage adaptations of Philip K. Dick's *Do Androids Dream of Electric Sheep?* and Ursula Le Guin's *The Lathe of Heaven* at the 3LD Art + Technology Center (adaptor and director); and original translations of Aristophanes' *Lysistrata* and Euripides' *Iphegenia in Aulis*. He is the author of numerous children's books, including *Paradox in Oz, The Living House of Oz, A Very Improbable Story*, and *Fractions in Disguise*.

VLADIMÍR MORÁVEK BIOGRAPHY

Vladimír Morávek is a theater and film director, based in Brno. He has been Artistic Director of Divadlo Husa na provázku (Theater Goose on a String) since 2005. Theater credits include *King Lear*, *Hamlet*, an adaptation of Miloš Foreman's *The Fireman's Ball*, and the Czech Chekhov project. Film credits include *Boredom in Brno* (screenplay) and *Hrubeš and Mareš, Friends Come Rain or Shine* (writer/director). He has also directed over 70 documentaries for television, as well as three television dramas.

VÁCLAV HAVEL BIOGRAPHY

Václav Havel first came to world attention as a playwright. Events and the power of his ideas launched him into the role of dissident, political prisoner, revolutionary, and finally, the President of Czechoslovakia (and later of The Czech Republic). Yet throughout the world-altering events that placed him in the center of history, Havel felt that his essential calling was still the same: he was a man of the theater, a writer of absurdist drama.

Havel was born in 1936 to a wealthy family, yet his privileges were quickly stripped away by the Communist regime that took power after World War II. His family's property was confiscated and he was forced to attend trade school, continuing his academic studies on his own. After a stint in the army, Havel began his theater career as a stagehand at the ABC Theatre.

From there, he moved to Theatre on the Balustrade, where he saw his work onstage for the first time: first a few comic sketches, and then his first full-length production, *The Garden Party*. That play along with *The Memo* established his international reputation as a playwright. He briefly thrived during Prague Spring in 1968, a program of reform whose slogan was "socialism with a human face." During that time, he travelled to New York for the premiere of *The Memo* (then translated as *The Memorandum*) at the Public Theater. It was to be his last chance to leave the country for more than 20 years.

In Prague, Russian tanks rolled in and with them came a far more repressive regime. Suddenly, Havel found his work banned and himself isolated. He also found himself in legal conflict with the "anti-parasite" laws, which stated that one could be jailed for not working. Havel eventually chose to take a job at a brewery, which he preferred as an alternative to his new isolation.

Now his plays were performed in friend's living rooms instead of on stage, but their influence was undiminished. They were distributed via *samizdat*, and a recording of Havel and his friend Landovsky reading the play *Audience* — a semi-autobiographical account of his time in the brewery — became so popular that people could be heard in cafes quoting it. Essays followed, including his seminal "Power of the Powerless," which articulated his credo that "living in truth" would contribute to the fall of Czechoslovakia's "post-totalitarian" government.

His political profile grew when he co-authored Charter 77, a human rights manifesto inspired, in part, by the Helsinki Accords. This soon led to his arrest and imprisonment. He remained in prison for four and a half years, with his only respite being the weekly, tightly proscribed letters to his wife, Olga. Those letters, with coded references to obscure philosophy that Havel included to slip his ideas past the censors, were gathered and published in a book called *Letters to Olga*.

After his release, Havel continued to be monitored by the police, at times in almost comical ways. During one vacation across Czechoslovakia, the secret police car that was trailing him got stuck in a ditch, and Havel stopped to help.

After they were rescued, the police followed him to his friends' house, arrested him and took him to the local jail for two days before releasing him.

In the meantime his writing continued, with more plays about his alter ego Ferdinand Vaněk, first introduced in *Audience,* followed by a string of other works on the state of Czechoslovak society, including *Largo Desolato* and *Temptation.* Vaněk became so popular that friends used the character in their own plays, a practice that continues to this day. Indeed, there may not have been such a popular and effective representative for the need for political change since Beaumarchais' Figaro.

By the end of the 1980s, Communism was collapsing. The Berlin Wall fell, and on November 17, 1989, what would be known as Czechoslovakia's Velvet Revolution began. Havel quickly became its de facto leader. The revolutionaries established their headquarters in The Magic Lantern Theatre. Within two months, the old regime was overthrown, and Havel found himself suddenly, and by his own account reluctantly, in the role of President. In Wenceslas Square, he famously declared "Truth and love must defeat lies and hatred," and indeed, it seemed at last to be so.

Havel served both as Czechoslovakia's last president and as The Czech Republic's first president, when in 1993 Slovakia chose to secede. While in office, he refused to be connected to any political party or movement. Inevitably, he had his detractors as well his supporters. His style as president was unconventional. He surrounded himself with artists even then, having a costume designer create new military uniforms, and asking Frank Zappa to be a political consultant.

After his wife Olga died, he grew ill with lung cancer. Part of his lung was removed, and he was nursed back to health by the actress Dagmar Veškrnová, whom he later married. This too was the cause for some public dissatisfaction, as his first wife was well loved.

Throughout his presidential career, he continued to advocate "living in truth," that is, finding a way to combine the moral and the political. He helped dissolve the Warsaw Pact, and he was a champion of human rights worldwide.

His work on human rights continued after the presidency, but he also returned to his artistic work. During the 2006 Havel Festival in New York, he revisited his complete works, and soon after he wrote his first new play in 20 years, *Leaving*, about a man forced to leave political office. A film of *Leaving* followed, which he directed. In what turned out to be his final work, he took an old dialogue, *The Pig*, and, in collaboration with Vladimir Morávek, combined it with Smetana's *Bartered Bride* to create a full production for the 2010 Theatre World Brno festival.

He was planning yet another play in December 2012 when he passed away at the age of 75. Three days of mourning were observed in the Czech Republic, and artists and politicians again mixed as both paid tribute to his lasting legacy.